TRUE
STYLE

A Look Beyond the Surface

by Glenda K. Harrison
Illustrated by Allison Taylor

True Style: A Look Beyond the Surface

Glenda K. Harrison

ISBN: 1537497715
ISBN-13: 9781537497716

While the rest of us stayed within the confines of our employer's dress code, "Katie" bent the rules by blending her own lifestyle and taste with the store's latest trends. She proved clothing alone was not the cornerstone to having style.

Je ne sais quoi

IN 1986, AFTER SPENDING TWO exciting years as a marketing and merchandising student, I graduated from the prestigious Fashion Institute of Design & Merchandising in Los Angeles. Like many with a great love for fashion, and the inner workings of the industry, I began my budding career as a manager for a popular retail clothing store. I was thrilled to work in an environment that allowed me to assist customers with their wardrobe needs, as well as being up close and personal with fashion on a daily basis. It was also during this time I became acutely aware of the considerable difference between fashion and style.

As a store manager, part of my job description was to make sure the staff adhered to the strict company dress policy. Each season we were provided with steep discounts to ensure we dressed in the current garments sold in the store. In essence, we became fashion clones with only subtle variances to our ensembles. In spite of the lack of diversity with our dress, there was one employee named "Katie" who marched to the beat of her own sartorial drum. Katie was a fashion renegade.

During the late 80s, we succumbed to an over-the-top trend which consisted of larger than life shoulder pads, bold pattern and color combinations, and colossal hair styles. Does the cast of Dynasty ring a bell? Though Katie wasn't a part of this popular quagmire of a trend, I found her fashion choices intriguing. On any given day she wore a slew of black rubber-band bracelets on her arm; her hair was usually styled in a messy ponytail; and with the exception of a red lip, she wore little to no makeup; vintage rock n' roll t-shirts; and the crème de la crème were a pair of black Doc Marten boots in which she had the uncanny ability to rock with just about everything she wore. Though the grunge look hadn't yet been introduced to pop culture (it wouldn't until the early 90s), Katie had given us a glimpse into what the - *I don't give a damn what you think* lifestyle entailed. There was a badass quality to Katie, yet, I found myself caring about her wellbeing. In spite of her tough exterior, she had a vulnerable and enduring quality – one in which I felt her armory was penetrable, and she needed to be protected.

While the rest of us stayed within the confines of our employer's dress code, "Katie" bent the rules by blending her own lifestyle and taste with the store's latest trends. She proved clothing alone was not the cornerstone to having style. Her fashion selections were viewed as unconventional, yet, her choices allowed us to peek into her world. It was obvious she wasn't a woman who needed to blend with the rest of society. Katie had a certain je ne sais quoi – a certain something that extended beyond the clothes she wore. She didn't care about the latest fashion trends; and whether she meant to or not, she shined from the inside-out by being genuine and representing herself authentically.

Time and time again, style is cast into a one dimensional story – usually referring to fashion, or one's fashion sense, often being relegated into this type of statement - *I like your style*, when in fact, style is much more complex than our sartorial pursuits. It is an intangible quality with a meaning far deeper than what the eye can see. True style speaks for us and has the ability to connect others to our internal depth.

When I first toyed with the idea of writing about style, I wondered how I would translate a subject with such depth, into a word with a clear understanding and meaning. I knew the task would be difficult, but I am passionate about the topic, and found myself needing to tackle it straight on. Since style has such a multi-layered meaning, I've written this book, not as a guide, but to create a point of understanding for such a complex subject.

How do I describe an innate, intangible quality one possesses – a certain je ne sais quoi (a certain something; uniqueness) that isn't manufactured? As a fulltime author, freelance style contributor, and all-around style enthusiast, who spends a great deal of time enveloped within the fashion scene, it has come to my attention, style, like certain words in the fashion language, is over-used, and often used in a single-layered context. Countless books have been written about style; however most have cemented the word within a one dimensional meaning relating to sartorial outcomes.

When I cross paths with a person who embodies that certain magical element, rarely am I solely captivated by their attire, rather, my curiosity is spurred by a more intrinsic element, and sparks a much deeper emotion. In the first encounter, it may be difficult to pinpoint the root of the attraction, nonetheless, it is present, and it inspires me to want to get to know more about them. A person who has the gift of harnessing their style manages to entice the admirer into wanting to go beyond the surface, and into a place that introduces us to their character. A mere scratching of the surface is not enough, you're intrigued, and now you want to know more.

With each chapter, we will remove the layers, uncovering and revealing the important qualities of this mysterious virtue called style. Once you have completed the book, you'll grasp the artistry of the word – like a beautiful tapestry, when the complete picture is woven, it becomes a lovely vision to behold – one with depth, color, and substance. Let's get started unveiling the true meaning. You'll never view style the same again.

Table of Contents

Introduction Je ne sais quoi · · · · · · · · · · · · · · · · · ·vii

Layer 1   Sartorial Pursuits · 1
          Sartorial Types · 2
          The Anti-Fashion · 4
          Closet Discrimination versus
          Closet Consumption· 6
          Fashion Robotism · 7
          Fashion Personality· 8
Layer 2   Know Thyself ·13
          Confidence ·15
          An Embraced History ·16
          Clarity ·16
          Valuable ·17
          No Copies Needed ·18
Layer 3   Be Unique · 21
          The Purpose of Butterfly Wings · · · · · · · · · · · 23
Layer 4   Be Authentic · 27
          Audrey Hepburn· 29
          Jacqueline Kennedy Onassis · · · · · · · · · · · · · 30
          Michelle Obama · 30

Layer 5   Be Your Style Story · 34
           Audrey Hepburn· 36
           Jacqueline Kennedy Onassis · · · · · · · · · · · · 37
           Michelle Obama · 38
Layer 6   Beyoutiful ·41

           Conclusion Be Integrated · · · · · · · · · · · · · · · · ·47
           About the Author ·51

True Style: A Look Beyond the Surface is dedicated to the "Katie's" in the world. Thank you for being a beautiful tapestry for all of us to behold.

There is an overriding contrast that separates those who embody great style with their fashion choices from the rest of the population.

Sartorial Pursuits

As I POINTED OUT IN the Introduction, the meaning of style is often kept within the realm of clothing, and since the purpose of this book is to go beyond the surface layer, let me first begin by discussing the outer layer - our sartorial pursuits. I would be amiss if I said our sartorial pursuits were not a part of our overall style, because it most certainly is a contributing factor. However, let me reiterate, clothing isn't the only, nor is it the main factor in determining true style – it is merely a part of a larger story.

When we set out to begin the day, before heading out into the public, the first activity we engage in is getting dressed. There is an overriding contrast that separates those who embody great style with their fashion choices from the rest of the population. The Katie's of the world manage to use their clothing as a form of self-expression, while others are simply getting dressed. In the latter, dressing is void of personal explanation, and is a task done out of obligation or consumption. To better explain the differences, I've divided the sartorial types into three categories: the Expressionist, the Obligationist, and, the Consumptionist.

Sartorial Types

The Expressionist

An Expressionist is an artist whose creative work captures sensitivity and imagination (thefreedictionary.com). I found this definition to be the most effective way to explain how a Katie navigates her closet. A prolific artist, she sees herself as a blank canvas, and is acutely aware of her emotions and the mood she wishes to convey and create through her clothing. Just like any great storyteller, the message she conveys is told with beautiful symmetry, and is able to draw the viewer into her world. Her wardrobe doesn't succumb to the latest fashion trends because she isn't interested in being a fashionista. Instead, a Katie selects garments that are authentic to her lifestyle, whether they're the latest trends or not. She doesn't buy fashion for the sake of it being in fashion. In essence, the Expressionist runs with the anti-fashion crowd. A group you'll seldom see standing in the long lines during the early morning hours for the release of the latest designer brand collaboration at a popular chain store. She would rather spend her time hunting for a one of a kind vintage treasure at a flea market, or creating a statement around a bequeathed brooch from her grandmother. A Katie has a meticulous eye and knows how to decipher whether a particular fashion should be added to her wardrobe, or whether it should remain on the rack. Additions to her closet are of great importance, and must blend effortlessly with the rest of her wardrobe, and into the life she lives. In the eyes of a Katie, fashion is an extended form of self-expression.

THE OBLIGATIONIST

For the Obligationist, dressing is mostly utilitarian. There typically isn't an emotional connection with their wardrobe, so clothing is simply viewed as the avenue used to cover the naked body. The idea of fashion iconography, as a way to interpret your life through the garments you wear, has no bearing on the Obligationist whatsoever. Because this person isn't emotionally invested in their wardrobe, there's often a disconnection between the image they project through their clothing, and how they truly wish to be perceived in the public. The Obligationist often considers dressing as a troublesome and daunting task. This mindset stems from a variety of reasons, though not limited to these few – thoughts on fashion as a frivolous act of consumption; not understanding how fashion relates to personal identification; or even having low thoughts of one's self. All of these factors play a contributing role into the mind of the Obligationist, and unfortunately, this blasé attitude toward getting dressed often reflects in how they present themselves through their sartorial pursuits.

THE CONSUMPTIONIST

As soon as the big announcement is made for the latest designer collaboration at a trendy store, the Consumptionist marks it on her calendar. She wouldn't miss this unveiling if her life depended on it. By all means necessary, she'll find a way to make it to the launch - even if it requires skipping work! The goal of the Consumptionist is to be one of the first to wear the latest look, and to share her purchases with the world. Unlike the Expressionists, the Consumptionist doesn't have time to relate to her clothes on a personal level, nor does she understand the blasé attitude of the Obligationist. She is too busy racking up copious amounts of the latest trends. If fashion insiders announce peacock feather head dresses as the new black, you better believe the Consumptionist will find a place for such an item in her wardrobe. The shopping habits of the Consumption are in direct opposition to the Expressionist. While the Expressionist strives to have a well curated wardrobe by carefully analyzing the fashion and determining what will work in her life, the Consumptionist views fashion as an avenue to constantly reinvent one's self as a reason to consume.

Most likely you'll identify with one of these three sartorial types. The three types are very different from each other, which gives further explanation into why there is such a wide inconsistency between people on the subject of getting dressed. For the purpose of this compelling subject, and to understand true style, the Expressionist is the idea sartorial type.

THE ANTI-FASHION

What made Katie stand out considerably was her total disregard to the fashion norms. She undoubtedly took an individual approach when it came to getting dressed. While the rest of the store employees failed to deviate from what was expected, Katie bucked the store's systematic dress code. She remained true to herself, by melding the seasonal trends with her own sartorial aesthetic. Katie was the Anti-Fashion, and for this, she was greatly admired.

Please don't view the term Anti-Fashion as a form of disrespect. By no means am I rallying the troops against an industry that has brought me so much joy and satisfaction. When I use this term, I use it with the utmost respect to the person I describe. I'm referring to someone who moves away from the predictable in their fashion choices. This individual approach to getting dressed is eloquently done because, to the anti-fashion, it isn't interesting to follow pop culture or a popular fashionista. What is more interesting is taking the time to scrutinize the fashions to determine what will undeniably represent them.

Possessing the Anti-Fashion mindset enables a person to shop for clothing, or attend fashion shows with a discerning eye. Watching the runway with the anticipation of creating an endless shopping list isn't important. What is important is having a penchant to carefully analyze the collections. In other words, becoming a slave to fashion trends is taboo. The Anti-Fashion is quite content with walking away with absolutely nothing – if need be necessary. Am I saying she never has the desire to buy what's on trend? Of course she will! But as I stated earlier, expression plays a vital part in the decision process, so if she connects with a trend, and can freely express herself, then chances are, she'll make a place for it in her life.

"Since the Expressionist embodies the Anti-Fashion way of thinking, opening her closet also unveils her carefully crafted and well curated point of view."

Notice I stated - *she'll make a place for it in her life.* When discussing the Anti-Fashion's shopping habits, it's necessary to make a clear distinction between closet discrimination and closet consumption. She takes great pride in asking herself - *How does this particular fashion relate to my life story, or am I adding a piece that fails to express my personality or individuality?* Since the Expressionist embodies the Anti-Fashion way of thinking, opening her closet also unveils her carefully crafted and well curated point of view.

CLOSET DISCRIMINATION VERSUS CLOSET CONSUMPTION

The biggest misconception about style is to believe it's achieved by wearing the hottest looks. This is where the great debate comes into play – Does *Having Style* equate to *Being in Style?* As you'll see, the two are not mutually exclusive.

As we're now beginning to understand, a person with an innate sense of style is very discriminating with what she chooses to wear. She realizes her clothing does not write her complete narrative, rather, like an intricately embroidered tapestry, her clothing, and all her other attributes, come together to form a beautifully integrated story. In the event she mistakenly purchases an outfit or garment that doesn't suit her, she'll feel like something isn't quite right. Therefore, it is vital she chooses wisely, and continues to exercise closet discrimination.

"The desire to make their fashion prowess known is evident by their insatiable need to add the latest trends to their closet."

A person who practices closet consumption is often a slave to the fashion trends, and has the tendency to band together the idea of *having style* with *being in style*. The desire to make their fashion prowess known is evident by their insatiable need to add the latest trends to their closet. There are other reasons why a person consumes on this high level, but for the purpose of this book, I'll remain within the confines of getting dressed. A person who shops for closet consumption believes their style quota is increased each time they step into the public arena wearing the hottest look. The use of a discerning eye is often cast aside. If in the past, lime green has been a sore point in this person's life, the opinion will change if color experts, Pantone Inc., selects lime green as the fashion color of the year. Without giving the new hot hue a second thought, it's off to the races in search of anything and everything lime green. After all, she now believes her lime green suit gives her an instant pass into having style. Au contraire, she may be on trend, but the depth in meaning of true style still manages to elude.

When the difference between Closet Discrimination and Closet Consumption is understood and adopted, a more fulfilling and transformative relationship between person and attire becomes easier to obtain. It's important to move beyond the common notion of eager clothing acquisitions in order to reach the point where the wardrobe puts the exclamation point at the end of your incredible story.

FASHION ROBOTISM

Fashion Robotism is the term I coined in reference to the basic, almost mundane way of dressing which lacks any type of personality, imagination or emotion, and is usually dictated by someone other than you – *This is what you should wear at this age, or this is how you should dress for this occasion.* With the digital world of blogging at the forefront of available wardrobe advice, it's quite easy to succumb to Fashion Robotism. Many fashion bloggers have built their entire platform with this point of view in mind – *This is how I dress, therefore you should too.* Delivering this type of fashion message is simple and doesn't require a person to have to think beyond what is visible to the eye. Unfortunately, Fashion Robotism is in total disregard to the individual personality or needs, and it drives people further away from connecting with their true self.

It has been almost four years since I launched my style blog, So What to Twenty. I knew from the beginning I wanted the content to have substance combined with visual expression. As my blog evolved, I saw fit to inspire my readership with stories about life situations while using my sartorial choices as the visual picture. It has always been important for me to inspire my readers to take an introspective journey in viewing fashion as an all-encompassing vehicle, and to explore their personal gifts, inner beauty, and, most importantly, a relationship with self.

"Style without substance is just getting dressed."

One of my readers said it best when she stated, *"Style without substance is just getting dressed."* I'm a firm believer in her statement. There is so much more to each of us than the obvious outer layer, and often times, the outer layer doesn't represent who we really are on the inside, or vice versa. Taking the precious time to get to know you unveils an incredible cornucopia of qualities – qualities which can draw you closer to determining your fashion personality.

FASHION PERSONALITY

Over the decades, the term Fashion Personality has made appearances in magazines, blogs, questionnaires, etc. What is a Fashion Personality? In layman terms – It's how you dress to express who you are. However simple the meaning may be, the idea of dressing to express who you are requires just that – knowing who you are. On my blog, So What to Twenty, I wrote a post titled, Knowing Your Fashion Personality 101, which was a close observation into how I came to understand my clothing choices through my fashion personality. Let's take a closer look:

> *I refer to my fashion personality as classic with a touch of bohemian, a bit of quirk, splashes of South Western influences, and the retro looks from the 60s and 70s era. Here is how I ultimately arrived to this conclusion: I'm a native Southern Californian (South West), born in the late 60s. The spirit of my homeland courses through my veins. Though I think highly of traditions (classic), I also am a person who connects with the earth. I live my life connected to the art community (bohemian). When I'm surrounded by nature and arts, I feel my best. The best way to describe how I feel is free, uninhibited, and at peace. Also, the idea of fashion non-absolutes (quirk) fascinates me.*

As you can see, my fashion personality is quite unique; it doesn't come from a fashion rule book, and is completely me. That which I'm passionate about; inspires me; and allows me to be myself are the forefront of my analysis, and assist with my self-expression. Now let's take a look at a fictitious person named Jenny. Though Jenny isn't real, per se, there may be others who can relate to this scenario:

> *Fifteen years ago Jenny graduated from a prestigious school of the arts as a dance major. However, do to unforeseen circumstances and financial obligations, she took a job as a bank teller, and eventually worked her*

way up the corporate ladder and into an executive position. Although the majority of Jenny's time is spent in a corporate environment that requires a strict dress code, she enjoys spending her free time volunteering as an instructor at a local dance academy. Jenny's life has been built around the income from her bank position, but she feels inspired by the free-spirited bohemian life, and still dreams of becoming a dancer.

Based on Jenny's story, some would suggest she falls into a classic fashion personality since the majority of her time is consumed by her career. However, if you read between the lines, Jenny's heart and true spirit is held within the arts community where she feels inspired and most like her true self. Does this make Jenny a classic personality, or a bohemian? The answer to the question is held within Jenny, and is the reason why a person has to do some soul-searching to discover the truth. Nine times out of ten, the true fashion personality comes into fruition when a person is very honest with whom they are on the inside. Jenny is obviously excelling in her banking career, and she may spend a hefty portion of her time in classic, navy sheath dresses and pumps, but the depth of her soul is bohemian – a place where she feels alive.

A careful look at Jenny suggests a woman who has surrendered to a way of dressing that's aligned with Fashion Robotism rather than personal identity; which leads me back to the Introduction and the story of Katie. Katie was presented with how she *should* dress (according to the corporate dress code), but remained true to herself by managing to combine her grunge lifestyle with the current trends of the store. What a novel idea, right? I bet Jenny would feel more like herself if she found a way to incorporate her bohemian spirit into her corporate life. I understand the two personalities are on opposite ends of the fashion spectrum; however it can be done by adding unique and subtle touches. Who knows, perhaps these minor wardrobe additions will inspire Jenny to make a leap of faith and live her life according to her passion.

Jenny's story is a prime example why many feel unlike themselves in their wardrobes. Strict dress codes, pressure from society, others dictating our norm, self-esteem, and fear of acknowledging who we are, all play a vital part in missing the mark in our sartorial pursuits. So I ask you, dear friend – What makes your heart sing? What era/decade do you most identify? What is your passion? What type of clothing silhouettes/fabrications/textures most resonate with you? Is there a culture or region you relate to the most? These are the types of questions you should ask yourself in order to discover your fashion personality. Remember, however you choose to paint your canvas, make sure the beautiful painting represents you.

Knowing yourself on an intimate level unleashes a bouquet of positive outcomes into your life, and onto the people who surround you. It's not difficult to recognize a person with this quality. There seems to be an undeniable confidence in the way they project themselves to the world.

Know Thyself

*"It takes more courage to find out who you are, by
examining the dark corners of your own soul, than
it does for a soldier to fight on the battle field."*

– William Butler Yeats

I CAN WRITE A SERMON on the less than positive results that can occur
when you live your life inauthentic, and with the attempt to try
to please others. Out of fear, conformity, and esteem issues, I
existed in this state of anguish for a great portion of my life. I felt
as if I wore a mask to conceal my true identity. Unfortunately, as I
grew more accustomed to my mask wearing alter-ego, it became
more difficult to remove the darn thing, and over time, I lost sight
of the real me. Before the mask grew completely attached, tiny
glimpses appeared sporadically from beneath. However, as time
moved forward, this false person began to take precedence over
the true, but fast fading one, and eventually, eclipsed the real
woman altogether.

After years of painful life experiences, somehow, the whirlwind of disappointments caused the mask to make a slight shift, revealing tiny, albeit significant details about the original woman and her dreams. Thank goodness I still held sketchy memories of myself before the disguise was put into place. The details which peeked from behind the camouflage were small, yet, they were distinct enough to awaken something powerful from within – a deep desire to finally become the woman I always craved. I decided it was necessary to take up the grueling task of ridding myself from the cumbersome mask. If I was to see myself once again, live my life at peace, and with a greater understanding of my value, the work had to be done.

As I toiled to excavate the pieces of my life, like a ghostly whisper, fragments of my dreams and hopes began to quietly resurface in my mind – *Get back to your love of writing and fashion. You are unique.* The whispers were faint, but their fervor stirred my soul, and pushed me to drive the shovel deeper into the soil. With each level of dirt removed, disparity was replaced with hope, and eventually, freedom arose from the earth and manifested an unmatched eagerness to fly. You can read more about my journey to self-discovery in my inspirational memoir titled, *A Place Called Peace.*

Rather than scraps I should toss by the wayside, I realized each of the fragmented pieces of my life were crucial elements in telling my story. Once I had them removed from the earth, I began the painstaking process of analyzing their meaning and weaving them together. When the tapestry had finally taken shape, I was able to stand back and behold what lay before me - no longer hidden beneath a self-induced façade; I now had the vigor to live this new promising life.

Knowing yourself on an intimate level unleashes a bouquet of positive outcomes into your life, and onto the people who surround you. It's not difficult to recognize persons with this quality. There seems to be an undeniable confidence in the way they project themselves to the world. This is understandable since intimacy with one's self requires a much deeper level of thought – personally as well as pertaining to others. There isn't a haughty arrogance, but a radiance that enraptures the people who have the pleasure of being in their company.

With this assurance comes a respect for your personal value and gifts. Your gifts, though they may not be unique per se, because you're a unique person, it qualifies them as such. Your gifts become your shield of armor and your roadmap in life. Because you have such a strong grip on your reality, and who you are, you're not willing to settle for anything less than what is on your radar. You know settling takes you off course and may lead you away from your calling. Without knowing your gifts, you may find yourself living behind the unwanted mask in a life of fakery. The mask isn't protection, rather a deceptive device that keeps you from living to your fullest potential. Remember - true style can only occur when a person is unmistakably living a life that resonates with their spirit and aspirations.

Here are five (5) reasons why knowing yourself on an intimate level will segue into having a more defined and fulfilling life:

CONFIDENCE

Having confidence is such an empowering life-force. When you have it, you become self-assured regarding your ability. Sure, you may initially feel frightened for taking on new endeavors; however, because confidence ignites a sense of strength, you realize stepping out into the unknown may lead to greater opportunities and increased fulfillment, for yourself, and the people in your life.

AN EMBRACED HISTORY

There are many quotes which suggest *forgetting the past in order to move forward into the future.* I beg to differ. As a matter of fact, I believe the opposite to be true. If you come from a less than stellar past, taking the steps to face prior experiences can lead to freedom, and a greater understanding of who you have become. With each life experience, whether good or bad, there will always be nuggets of wisdom to take from it. As with everything we encounter in our day-to-day lives, true growth occurs when there is stress and pressure, or when situations become uncomfortable. As an example, when a person aspires to reshape their physique, heavy weights are used to stretch and challenge the muscles. Such is the case for our lives. The weights represent all the pressure, turmoil, setbacks and obligations we have to face. If we choose to hide from them, there wouldn't be a learning experience, and therefore, the life muscle will remain unfit. My advice is to pick up the weights in life, from the past and the future, and use them to your advantage – a sculpted life of self-awareness.

Always remember - your past is a portion of your history. Hiding from your past won't make it disappear. In fact, the more we try to mask yesteryear, the more it can unwittingly wreak havoc on our today. Realizing and accepting how history comes together with the present is a sure sign of maturity, and a gained appreciation of your journey.

CLARITY

During the 2016 summer Olympics in Rio de Janeiro, Brazil, I watched as Michael Phelps (USA medalist) sat in the waiting room for his turn to compete in one of his many swim events.

At one point, while waiting for the race to begin, cameras caught South African swimmer, Chad le Clos, trying to break Phelps' concentration. Clos tried his best to distract Phelps by boxing in front of him, and leering in his direction. In spite of Clos' intentions, Phelps won the race, and soon thereafter, media sources began to circulate a photo of Clos looking into the next lane at Phelps during the race. A disheartening conclusion for Clos, but for Phelps, his clarity and intentions were very clear. He knew why he was competing, and wasn't willing to let distractions stop him from achieving his goal. While Phelps was focused on winning the entire race, his competitor lost sight of the bigger picture and focused strictly on Phelps.

What an incredible life lesson. It's important to steer clear from distractions, and remain focused on your goal. When you know yourself, it becomes easier to focus on distant goals and ambitions. You've come to grips with your past and have embraced it; there's no more denying of yourself; you're confident in the person you've become; and you've set a new vision for your future. The next step is to sharpen your focus and begin moving in the direction of that which you hope to achieve. Having clarity is dynamic and offers directional steps to your destination. Your eyes are open to what's on the horizon. Though all aspects of your hopes are yet to come into focus, you're confident in the steps you've taken. You know the path laid before you was created exclusively for you.

VALUABLE

When I refer to value, I'm not writing about dollar amounts, or ethics, rather the powerful details in your life that motivates you, and gives you purpose. Your value is the cornerstone of your life, and gives the base for what all areas of your life are built upon. The cornerstone, or your value, is what's necessary for building a solid foundation. When you know your value, there are a variety of benefits to your everyday life:

1. You won't easily fall prey to unwanted situations since your values are characterized by what's important to you;
2. You live with intention rather than unintentionally. Therefore it becomes much easier to accomplish what's necessary on a day to day basis;
3. Your life is lived authentically because your values are the driving force behind your journey;
4. You feel energized because your values allow you to live purposeful;

No Copies Needed

The game changer in the process of obtaining personal intimacy is when you realize there's no need to look at the lives of others for direction on what to do next. I'm not saying you won't seek wisdom or advice, but asking others for their opinions on what you should do with your life becomes a thing of the past. You're so comfortable with who you've become, you no longer have the desire to mimic the lives of others, nor are you susceptible to trying to please anyone but yourself.

> *"...a copy is merely a copy, and is only a one dimensional impersonation incapable of satisfying the full scope of the object it tries to mimic - the emotions, education, passion, experiences, and history that makes a person unique."*

When a person lacks definition and direction, unfortunately, with this world of massive digital accessibility, it's easy to become mesmerized by the life of others; especially when that life appears exciting or simple to achieve. Right before our eyes, the seemingly perfect life is laid before us, and if you don't have a firm foundation in the direction you're headed, it can be easy to fall victim to patterning your life after someone else. The underlying issue with copying is this - a copy is merely a copy, and is only a one dimensional impersonation incapable of satisfying the full scope of the object it tries to mimic - the emotions, education, passion, experiences, and history that makes a person unique. It's perfectly fine to admire others, but trying to mirror, or chasing someone's rainbow without knowing your own likes and dislikes, or understanding each person has their own personal journey; well, this can be a recipe for disaster.

As you're now beginning to understand, style is much more than what we choose to wear. Style relates to a person's internal depth, and how that depth harmonizes with external factors. It may sound confusing, but as we continue further into the remaining layers, it will become thoroughly understandable. Now that we have discovered je ne sais quoi, and have removed layer one - Know Thyself, let's continue exposing the other layers on our quest to revealing a person with true style.

Butterflies understand the unique quality of their wings. Your gifts, or butterfly wings, are specifically designed for you. You are an original, and not a copy of someone else. Embrace the beauty of your uniqueness.

Be Unique

IT'S BEEN OVER 30 YEARS since I worked with "Katie" in the trendy clothing store, and it is quite obvious she left an indelible impression on me. Like I stated previously, Katie didn't spend her money racking up the latest trends, or purchasing precious, high-end items, yet she dressed in a way that exhibited her uniqueness. I couldn't imagine Katie dressed head-to-toe in the trendy garb sold in the store. For Katie to feel her best, it was necessary to express her unique sartorial personality while still maintaining the store's dress code. This was a great accomplishment, and one which should have been celebrated by placing a congratulatory medal onto her grunge knit cap.

Unfortunately in today's hyper-voyeuristic society, many choose to exist in a realm consistent to one of Fashion Robotism – one that has been pre-ordained or pre-selected by someone other than you, and has very little to do with individuality. There are a variety of factors that contribute to this type of existence: upbringing, religion, culture, educational systems, etc.; can all lead to this type of de facto. Rather than subscribing to an individualistic approach in learning, it becomes easier for educational systems to bundle the students into a single, non-descriptive group. Instead of parents encouraging their children to bloom by strengthening their unique qualities; conformity often prevails. In other words, at a very early age, many are taught to assimilate, and don the mask, in place of embracing the beauty of differentiating ourselves. I have respect for our education system and our educators, and understand parents and caregivers who are trying to do their best with children; yet, it would be a novel idea to uplift someone for their uniqueness instead of burying the uniqueness in the sand.

Time and time again I have encountered someone without self-identified passions, trying to replicate the passion of another. The problem with this scenario is they can only *see* the love exuding from the original person. Attempting to garner the magic of someone else typically leads to a half-baked, unenthusiastic pursuit which is often seen by others as unnatural.

> *"A life lived celebrating your uniquely defined gift(s) propels you to live spirited and free from succumbing to the unwanted scrutiny of others."*

When a person's life purpose is rooted in their unique qualities, they most certainly stand out from the crowd. They project an allure which not only melds their fashion choices, but their entire essence as well. There's a joy that glows internally and beams throughout their entire being. The best way to achieve this type of liveliness is to seek out what's best suited for your life. A life lived celebrating your uniquely defined gift(s) propels you to live spirited and free from succumbing to the unwanted scrutiny of others.

There are self-evident reasons why it's vital to embrace your gifts (as I've stated), and there are points which aren't so obvious, but matter a great deal in how one can successfully navigate through life. Below are six points I discovered while searching for a better understanding for my life. During this precious time of self-discovery, my natural gifts were clearly identified. I also unearthed how the scientific purpose of the butterfly's unique wings parallel with the human necessity to utilize our God-given gifts. Here is what I discovered:

The Purpose of Butterfly Wings

1. ***Scientific Purpose***: Wings are crucial for a butterfly's survival. The wings are covered with veins that provide the creature with oxygen.
   My Discovery: Butterflies know their wings provide them with life. Not using their wings/gift will cause them to parish. Your gifts are your life support, and not using them will slowly cause you to die emotionally.

2. ***Scientific Purpose***: When the butterfly first emerges from the pupa, the wings are crinkled and wet. It then hangs upside-down and pumps blood into the wings to inflate them. Once the wings are dry, it can then fly.
   My Discovery: Butterflies patiently and strategically work toward using their wings. Don't become intimidated by your gifts. Embrace them. If you work hard and strive toward your goals, you will feel satisfied in completing them.

3. ***Scientific Purpose***: The wings distinguish the butterfly from other insects by providing identity and uniqueness.
   My Discovery: Butterflies understand the unique quality of their wings. Your gifts are specifically designed for you. You are an original and not a copy of someone else. Embrace the beauty of your uniqueness.

4. **Scientific Purpose**: The wings camouflage the butterfly against predators.
   My Discovery: Butterfly wings provide a shield of protection. The butterfly proudly spreads its wings when it sees a predator. There's no greater power than knowing your authentic self, or understanding and using your gifts. Your gifts are your strength and shield against anyone who may try to cause harm or devalue you.
5. **Scientific Purpose**: The wings attract a suitable mate.
   My Discovery: Butterfly wings are made from a variety of unique color combinations which make the creature recognizable by potential mates. Your gifts make you attractive to suitors. Know the value and power of your gifts will determine what you will or will not tolerate in a relationship.
6. **Scientific Purpose**: The wings are the butterfly's source of transportation and how it navigates through life.
   My discovery: Your life will make room for your gifts to be utilized. You can't live a life that was structured for someone else. Each of us has our own unique gifts and path to take. Living the life of someone else makes it hard to recognize and use your own gifts. When you know your uniqueness, you can navigate through life in your own direction.

This new and profound discovery clearly marked the beginning of my journey in using my natural gifts, or what I like to call – my butterfly wings (I'll share more about my unique gifts in Layer Six). Since spreading my wings, I feel an incredible freedom, and an ease in the direction my life has taken. I was once a woman who felt forced into the world I lived, while clinging to the hope of finding true meaning. Now, I revel in the depth of my identified uniqueness.

As we continue moving into the next layers, your understanding of how each quality relates to the next should be coming together. It makes perfect sense how je ne sais quoi melds into knowing thyself; and how having a personal intimacy can decode the power of your uniqueness – all of which are the building blocks to understanding true style.

When we delve into fashion history and draw inspiration from iconic
women, such as, Audrey Hepburn, Jacqueline Kennedy Onassis, and
First Lady of the United States, Michelle Obama, it's easy to recognize
how their authenticity encompasses their impeccable fashion sense.

LAYER 4

Be Authentic

AUTHENTICITY MAY BE THE MOST obvious layer to expose as it relates to possessing true style, and yet, it is the most difficult characteristic for people to embrace. Like we discussed in Layer Two (Know Thyself), we would rather don a mask than let anyone discover our true character. Living our lives in its truest form is scary and requires subjecting ourselves to vulnerability; and being vulnerable, to many, is a sure sign of weakness.

> *"When a person lives behind a mask, they begin to harbor a disingenuous quality. A tiresome game of 'hide but don't seek' is constantly played to con ceal the truth."*

I propose a question - Is vulnerability a sign of weakness? I believe the opposite to be true. When a person lives behind a mask, they begin to harbor a disingenuous quality. A tiresome game of 'hide but don't seek' is constantly played to conceal the truth. Eventually the elaborate game of hoax seeps into other areas, and eventually causing unwanted fractures to develop to the self-esteem. It becomes a life of drawn curtains, loneliness and despair – a sure sign of entering the pathway of a hidden truth.

27

On the other hand, when someone is open to being vulnerable, the fractures, though they may have been difficult to receive, become a part of their framework, and not something that must be hidden. There is a defining beauty and openness to the cracks that allows the warmth of the individual to shine through. The more time spent with this individual, the more you'll become engulfed by their refreshing disposition – a disposition that resonates as sincerity, and a sincerity which registers as authentic.

So I ask again - Is vulnerability a sign of weakness? Since we all have choices in the way we choose to live, I would rather be a person who lives authentically; acknowledges my past and shortcomings, and respects them as a part of my story. I can attest to the drawbacks of living an unauthentic life, for one, I always felt as if I was in search of a missing piece to the puzzle. It didn't matter what activity I engaged in, or who entered my life, the outcome was always the same – an itch I couldn't scratch. I tried to scratch the itch with just about every object imaginable without obtaining the results I needed. Finally, after much soul-searching, I realized the only way I could relieve the annoyance was to denounce life-plagiarism and to embrace all of me – cracks and all.

When a person chooses to adopt or portray a false persona, the sham will eventually unravel. All one has to do is spend time with the deceptive person and you'll be left scratching your head in wonder. Furthermore, the pretense has a way of divulging itself without warning, it sneaks in with a bullhorn to make the announcement the trickster may dread – *May I have your attention please...This person is a fake!* Whether this announcement is made publically, or internally, the results are painful and should be measured as a wake-up call to stop pretending and to embrace the person you are meant to be – a person with your own destiny, passions, journey, and with your own trail to blaze.

When authentic and style are carefully examined, the two topics are naturally conjoined, which would explain why it's difficult to declare one attribute without the other. How can one stake their claim in having style without having a bona fide connection with self? The meaning of style has now been revealed as having an ability to establish individuality or uniqueness through sartorial expression – an expression that would be impossible to achieve without the significant character trait of authenticity. In other words, true style can't exist without its notable comrade - authenticity.

When we delve into fashion history and draw inspiration from iconic women, such as, Audrey Hepburn, Jacqueline Kennedy Onassis, and First Lady of the United States, Michelle Obama, it's easy to recognize how their authenticity encompasses their impeccable fashion sense. Whether or not they utilized professional stylists, you can plainly see how their fashion choices clearly represent them in the truest form. Let's take a closer look at these three icons:

AUDREY HEPBURN

While embracing the strength of her femininity, Audrey Hepburn was the epitome of gamine chic. Famous for donning a pixie cut, a simple pair of slim-cut pants, ballet flats, and turtleneck sweater, or the most beautiful gowns by Hubert de Givenchy, she embodied a juxtaposition of tomboy cool with a twist of coquettish glamour. Yet, with all of her film accolades, there was a vulnerable quality which made Ms. Hepburn warm, likeable and very approachable. She gave the impression one could ask for her advice, and she would freely share her wisdom over a cappuccino.

JACQUELINE KENNEDY ONASSIS

When Jackie Kennedy was the First Lady, sophistication enveloped the White House. Though she seemed aloof, Jackie's fashion choices of brightly hued ensembles, clean lines with uncomplicated details, pill box hats, and opera gloves, managed to invite everyone into her exclusive world. During her White House years, Oleg Cassini was the designer for most of her enchanting looks. Though Cassini was the master creator, Jackie was the commander-in-chief for a majority of the creations. She insisted the creations represented her authenticity and position by showcasing her uniqueness, sense of taste, her love for art and history, and a woman of immense decorum.

MICHELLE OBAMA

Michelle Obama is the perfect example of the alpha female - the personification of strength, good character, grace, and authenticity. Since the day Michelle burst onto the scene with her equally charismatic husband, President Barak Obama, she hasn't wavered from her true character. Never has the United States had a First Lady who would be seen jumping rope with neighborhood children; taking on the latest dance moves on television; and publically demonstrating passionate love for her husband, while remaining a steadfast symbol of dignity. Mrs. Obama's fashion sense also represents her character and the life she lives. Throughout her time at the White House, she repeatedly wore creations from lesser known designers, which spoke of her desire to see everyone prosper and have their fair share. Because she's very much in tune with herself, her clothing choices always showcase her best physical features, and the true spirit of Michelle Obama.

With each of these iconic women, there is a thread that binds them together - this thread is authenticity. The statement, *There will never be another (Audrey, Jackie, Michelle)*, always makes its way into the conversation when speaking of them. They are genuine women who didn't allow a false persona to envelop their true character. As it pertains to their outward appearance, because of their firm foundation with self-identity, they were able to captivate the public with fashion choices that enhanced their stories in greater and precise detail.

Can you imagine Audrey assuming the life of Jackie, or Michelle imitating Audrey? As strange as this scenario may seem, it happens more often than one could imagine. Case in point, during the United States presidential conventions, the wife of a candidate, perhaps unwittingly, used Michelle Obama's convention speech as her own. The results weren't positive, not only because of the obvious blunder, but because the speech was the life journey and convictions of Mrs. Obama, and when it was used by another, it came across as insincere. This prime example of life-plagiarism took place on a grand scale and had awkward results. Imagine if the candidate's wife walked onto the stage and told her own story. My guess is she would have won the hearts of many for her bravery, and for being vulnerable. Yet, even when honesty has proven to be the best policy, this type of behavior continues to plague our psyche. Here are a few reasons why this type of behavior continues:

- Fear of being judged harshly for the past;
- Trying to maintain the level of standards governed by others;
- Lack of self-confidence;

- Genuine sense of feeling unhappy with your life;
- Not forming an intimate relationship with self.

In retrospect, here are the benefits associated with being authentic:

- The freedom of being yourself (flaws and all), rather than hiding from mistakes or trying to conceal flaws, they become a part of your story;
- An acute sense of knowing what works and what doesn't work for your life;
- More in tune to the direction you want to take in life;
- More relatable (People are drawn to relatable life stories);
- More confident in your decisions;
- There won't be room for negative people in your life;
- Selective with whose advice you'll take;
- Self-Confidence;
- Self-Respect

The benefits of living authentically extend far beyond the obvious. When you trust in the natural gifts you're equipped with; cultivating and massaging them along the way, and when you accept your *entire* story, your life will take on a new meaning – one which blankets you in freedom, has substance, and is ultimately defined by you.

To qualify as having true style, depth of character is vital; utilizing your voice is crucial; and accepting your story (past and present) is essential — a story without false pretenses or fabricated storylines, just pure unadulterated YOU.

Be Your Style Story

WHEN I ENTERED THE WORLD as a freelance style writer with my blog, So What to Twenty, from the onset, I knew I wanted my platform to reflect more than the conspicuous - *What I'm Wearing* type of posts. It was important for me to convey my character, and to bring history, depth and understanding to myself and fashion. I wanted my voice to extend beyond the obvious, and into the more expressive world of true style. With the meaning of style having a much greater expanse than clothing, I began to create Style Stories. With each style story, I tell narratives about life while using my fashion choices as the visual image. In addition, I made it a point to have the photo shoots in locations that further developed the story.

When I refer to stories, I'm referring to my unique and diverse journey; the message that intertwines my life, values, critical intelligence, spirituality, and purpose, or in other words, a genuine narrative. People are naturally attracted to what's genuine. By adopting the storyline of another, you then take on the behavior that many in our population subscribe to - a behavior that follows the norm, and provides little wiggle room within the restraints of a box. Naturally, this behavior blocks others from getting to know the real you. For a story to be received, it must come from the heart, and radiate truth while weaving a personal narrative. Those who are well received have a special allure, captivates an audience, and, whether they're aware or not, they have the ability to stir emotions. Undoubtedly, a person who has these reputable qualities will take their place in the arena of having the highest form of style – True Style.

Now that we have delved into the previous layers, the mark which qualifies true style is now beginning to take form. You see, dear friends, to think style requires nothing more than having an exquisite wardrobe, equates to style without substance, which is superficial thinking. Think back to the style icons discussed in layer four – Audrey Hepburn, Jacqueline Kennedy Onassis, and Michelle Obama. When you think of these women, sure, you'll remember the amazing way in which they dressed, but you'll also remember their stories, and the clever way in which they engaged the masses – a life that existed far beyond them carrying a popular handbag, or dazzling us with their exquisite ball gowns.

"Engaging stories are always weaved with victories and challenges. It is through these experiences we become relatable to the observer or listener. Beware of anyone who presents themself as superior or beyond fault; this is a sure sign of a fabricated story."

Once again, let's consider Audrey, Jacqueline and Michelle - These women contrast in comparison; however, what makes them simpatico is the engaging way in which they shared their story. They didn't attempt to echo the life of another by becoming a quasi-version of someone else; instead, they garnered praise with the skillfulness in which they communicated their message via dialog, sartorial, and by their presence. Let's take a quick look into their style stories:

AUDREY HEPBURN

* A childhood dampened by World War II;
* A desire to become a prima ballerina;
* A legendary career during the golden era of Hollywood;
* Her experience as a child during the war, propelled her to spend her final years as a humanitarian caring for the needy as a UNICEF Ambassador.

Audrey Hepburn's Sartorial Style Story: During her years on the silver screen, many of Ms. Hepburn's most iconic fashion moments (Funny Face, Sabrina and Breakfast at Tiffany's) were the creations of famed designer, Hubert de Givenchy. Givenchy's designs perfectly represented Ms. Hepburn. He was able to exhibit her playful and innocent charm, while mindfully displaying her coquettishness and glamour. Yet, in her private, off screen life, Audrey took on a more laid-back and down-to-earth approach in dressing by wearing basic pieces like simple sweaters, cigarette pants, loafers and ballerina flats – easy garments that were a tribute to her need to be unembellished and relaxed in private. In her final years as a UNICEF Ambassador, she was often photographed in simple polo shirts, denim or khakis, white sneakers, and her hair pulled back. A departure from her glamorous days in Hollywood, and a return to her simple upbringing.

JACQUELINE KENNEDY ONASSIS

- Ambitions to work in the field of journalism as a young adult;
- An elegant First Lady of the United States;
- Devoted mother, and wife to President John F. Kennedy;
- Strength and dignity she showed during the assassination of her husband;
- Continued to champion literature and the arts in her later years.

Jackie Kennedy Onassis' Sartorial Style Story: Jackie grew up as a debutant in America's high society and was accustomed to the finer things in life. Though she wore many designs from various couture houses, during her White House years she mostly preferred the custom creations by Oleg Cassini. With Cassini's unique designs, Mrs. Kennedy was seen as regal, and with a sense of culture, history and newness. His designs catapulted Jackie into the fashion icon status, resulting in women, all over the world, wanting to immolate her look. The Cassini/Jackie collaboration was pristine, intentional, had an almost architectural, yet artistic quality to the designs. After her years as the First Lady, and her marriage to Greek business tycoon, Aristotle Onassis, Jackie tried to live a discreet life in New York City. She was surrounded by literature, the arts, and all the things she loved. Jackie was often photographed by paparazzi donning a head scarf and dark, over-sized sunglasses – the perfect Do Not Disturb sign for a woman who hungered for privacy, and wanting to live life on her own terms.

MICHELLE OBAMA

* Inspired at an early age to excel in academics;
* Graduated from Princeton and Harvard Law where she met her future husband, Barak Obama, who would become the 44th President of the United States;
* Career in law;
* Mother of two daughters and a role model to women young and old;
* An advocate for healthy living

Michelle Obama's Sartorial Style Story: Michelle Obama grew-up with a drive and determination to succeed in academics, and in her career choices. In combination of her middle class upbringing and her position as the First Lady of the United States, she is clever with her ability to juxtapose high with moderate priced fashions. Her wardrobe was a perfect mix of mainstream brands mixed with top design houses. As top designers clamored for the opportunity to design Mrs. Obama's Election Day and inaugural attire, her modus operandi was to give lesser known designers the coveted positions. Overnight, designers like Jason Wu, Narciso Rodriguez, and Isabel Toledo, were made into household names. Her fashion choices were relatable, displayed her strong physique while enhancing her femininity, and were a perfect representation of her vivacious spirit.

Engaging stories are always weaved with victories and challenges. It is through these experiences we become relatable to the observer or listener. Beware of anyone who presents themself as superior or beyond fault; as this is a sure sign of a fabricated story. When we identify with someone on an intimate level, it's because their story is relatable; and, when a story is inspirational, it's by virtue of admiration. When the subject of a story is found to be both, *relatable* and *inspiring,* the powerful force, now known as True Style is awakened. The person who embodies true style reaches far beyond the superficial idea of style (which relates to outward appearances), and onto a coveted stage that shines for the world to see. To qualify as having true style, depth of character is vital; utilizing your voice is crucial; and accepting your story (past and present) is essential – a story without false pretenses or fabricated storylines, just pure unadulterated YOU.

...What was revealed were priceless treasures—my unique gifts that make me beyoutiful! Powerful words that give me depth and meaning (substance).

Beyoutiful

Beyoutiful: An interpretation of the word Beautiful, with the suggestive meaning - when a person lives to represent them self, it's indeed beautiful.

PEPPERED THROUGHOUT THE CHAPTERS OF True Style were clues that gave glimpses into the way I once lived. Like many, I sequestered myself behind a mask, and inside the confines of a box; too full of self-doubt to live the way I envisioned. As a young girl I devoured every fashion publication I could get my hands on. My greatest joy was soaking in all the pages of the glossy magazines. I sat and daydreamed about a life lived within the field of fashion. Though at an early age, I wasn't sure of a particular field in fashion, I simply wanted to be a part of the exciting sartorial world. Unfortunately as I advanced into my teenage years, I was bombarded with an ongoing negative commentary that eventually led to my climbing inside a box and securing the lid closed. Each time I mustered the courage to peek outside, the voice began to sling its hurtful dialog in my direction. Eventually I gave up the attempt to free myself, and shut the lid on my place of false security.

At the age of forty-seven I found myself at my wits end. Within a short period of time, the New Year brought with it a multitude of heartaches and challenges. One incident in particular, though it was very hurtful to experience, turned out to be my awakening, and the beginning to forming a new and lasting relationship with myself. With this new discovery, I entered into the biggest and most rewarding endeavor of my life - I undertook a systematical dismantling of my thoughts in order to reach a point where I was brave enough to climb out of the box for good. I leaped out of the box and snatched the mask off with such force; they disintegrated – never to be entered into or worn again.

"When you live beyoutifully, the fear of being found out is no longer a factor. You develop a strong desire to conquer the ambitions you once feared."

Peaceful is the best way to describe how I felt with my new found freedom. I felt like a butterfly unfurling my wings and taking flight for the very first time. Flying to these new heights gave a vantage point I had never seen before. I felt alive, conscious, enthusiastic, and yes, beyoutiful. No longer did the chains of self-doubt bind me, nor did I feel immobilized by fear, rather, I began to use fear as a guiding light. I took on the mantra - *If an idea scares me, I'll move in its direction.* And that's exactly what I did. When you live beyoutifully, the fear of being found out is no longer a factor. You develop a strong desire to conquer the ambitions you once feared. When you think about the new found emotions that go along with self-approval, the negative energy falls by the wayside, and you become aligned with all that makes you special and unique. In addition, the desire to move toward forgotten goals and dreams becomes a driving force.

During the dismantling of the barrier of negative discourse, I simultaneously began excavating buried facts about myself. As with any excavation process, once the items were discovered; the painstaking clean-up work began. Once the dirt was dusted away, what was revealed were priceless treasures - my unique gifts that make me beyoutiful – powerful words that give me depth and meaning (substance), and subsequently, acts as my personal identification. My gifts are unrelated to anyone's idea of me, and are much more profound than credentials associated with marital status, occupation, family history, hobbies, etc. To bring clarity to the importance of knowing your gifts, I would like to share mine with you:

Blessed: I honor my relationship with my Higher Power.

Trailblazer: I have an entrepreneurial spirit. I'm not afraid to tread new waters.

Promising: I work hard and passionately to achieve my goals.

Beautiful: This is not a statement of vanity, rather an introspective look inside my spirit.

Inspiring: My life and my words are encouraging to others.

Unique: I accept, embrace, and recognize the qualities that make me special.

Vulnerable: (Vulnerable was recently added to my list) I am a woman who doesn't deny the sharing of her hurts, pains, joys, and triumphs. Sharing these feelings and emotions with others is empowering and gives me strength.

By embracing my gifts, I am more directional and grounded to forge ahead with the ability to live a life designed by me. Does this mean I'm never tempted by doubt? Of course I am, but now it doesn't paralyze me as it once did. Instead, like I mentioned above, the doubt, which equates to fear, has become my guiding light. So, if disparaging comments are hurled in my direction, I now return the negative talk with my mantra - *If an idea scares me, I'll move in its direction.* Each time I rise to the occasion, a new and exciting pathway emerges for me to venture into.

I'm most certain you're wondering how my devised word, Beyoutiful, relates to true style. If you recall, back in Layer Three (Be Unique), I shared how the scientific purpose of a butterfly's unique wings parallels with the human necessity to utilize our own gifts. It's simple – without having the knowledge and charge to live freely in your uniqueness, you most certainly won't have the potency to possess true style. True style equals je ne sais quoi, and je ne sais quoi is segregated to people with an undeniable confidence in their uniqueness. These qualities give people substance, and this group understands why style without substance is just getting dressed. This final statement loops us around to Layer One (Sartorial Pursuits) and one of my opening statements - *our clothing isn't the only factor in determining our true style – it is merely a part of the bigger picture.*

In conclusion, living beyoutifully equates to an embraced life; living in the truest form; the acceptance of one's personal story; and operating with one's unique gifts. These components are beautifully conjoined to the meaning of true style, which is, **an integrated life - when all aspects, including wardrobe, are in harmony**. The masters of this extraordinary ability enrapture us with their intrinsic skill of weaving together each of these details to form a beautiful and intriguing work of art – the interwoven masterpiece called True Style.

A person who has mastered the gift of harnessing their true style
manages to entice the admirer into wanting to go beyond the surface,
and into a place that introduces us to their character.

Be Integrated

WE FINALLY REVEALED THE MULTI-LAYERED person who inhabits the world of True Style:

> *Living beyoutifully equates to an embraced life; living in the truest form; the acceptance of one's personal story; and operating with one's unique gifts. These components are beautifully conjoined to the meaning of* **True Style: an integrated life - when all aspects, including wardrobe, are in harmony.** *The masters of this extraordinary ability enrapture us with their intrinsic skill of weaving together each of these details to form a beautiful and intriguing work of art – the interwoven masterpiece called True Style.*

Having this depth of substance, makes it clear as to why I stated the following in the Introduction (Je ne sais quoi):

> *I've written this book of style, not as a guide, but to create a point of understanding for such a complex subject. When I cross paths with a person who embodies that*

certain magical element, rarely am I solely captivated by their attire, rather, my connection with them is more intrinsic, and sparks a much deeper emotion. Though it can be difficult to pinpoint the connection, it is there, and it inspires me to want to get to know them more intimately. A person who has mastered the gift of harnessing their true style manages to entice the admirer into wanting to go beyond the surface, and into a place that introduces us to their character. A mere scratching of the surface is not enough, you're intrigued, and now you want to know more about them. Once you have completed the book, it is my hope you'll grasp the artistry of the word – like a beautiful tapestry, when the complete picture is woven, it becomes a lovely vision to behold – one with depth, color, and substance.

Indeed the integration of the layers forms a beautiful tapestry, complete with depth, color, complexities, and a unique story. To integrate on this level requires an innate discernment, which collectively, many will not uncover in their lives; this explains why individuals with je ne sais quoi are rare beings. While the misconception of style may remain on the surface for the masses, writing this book proved to a refreshing reprise. Finally, after years of witnessing style discussed as merely clothing, or how one wears clothing, it feels sublime to finally explore beyond the surface and into the deeper meaning of True Style.

About the Author

FROM THE RUNWAY TO YOUR personal closet, be it advice on the proper attire, or suggestions on how to live life to the fullest, readers throughout the world are being inspired by connecting to *"So What to Twenty",* a style blog by creator, author, and freelance style contributor, Glenda K. Harrison, graduate of the Fashion Institute of Design & Merchandising in Los Angeles, California. The name, So What to Twenty, came about when Harrison decided she wanted to give a voice, and demonstrate the vitality in women over the age of twenty – an age which seems to be coveted by the fashion industry.

Although fashion and style are important to her, Harrison's real passion is reminding others of the importance of self-love and using one's God-given gifts and talents. Her blog inspires readers to view fashion as an all-encompassing vehicle and encourages women to explore their personal gifts, inner beauty, power, and most importantly, style. Harrison has been quoted saying, *"I view my clothing as the cast of characters in my life, and together we tell the story of Glenda."*

Harrison has authored an inspirational memoir titled, A Place Called Peace. She currently lives in Southern California with her husband and two sons.

Email   Glenda K. Harrison: glendak.style@yahoo.com
Website: GlendaKHarrison.com
Blog: sowhattotwenty.blogspot.com

About the Illustrator
Allison Taylor is an artist, graphic designer, and illustrator. A graduate from Texas State University with a Bachelor's in Communication Design, she has used her expertise working with multiple design firms, non-profit organizations, and most recently, fashion brands. Allison resides in Austin, Texas with her husband, Mike.